CRAFTS

OF THE MIDDLE AGES™

THE CRAFTS AND CULTURE OF A
MEDIEVAL MANOR

Joann Jovinelly and Jason Netelkos

The Rosen Publishing Group, Inc., New York

For Mom, a spirited and creative woman who taught me it was possible to make magic

Published in 2007 by The Rosen Publishing Group, Inc.
29 East 21st Street, New York, NY 10010

Library of Congress Cataloging-in-Publication Data

Jovinelly, Joann.
The crafts and culture of a medieval manor/Joann Jovinelly and Jason Netelkos.—1st ed.
   p. cm.—(Crafts of the Middle Ages)
Includes bibliographical references and index.
ISBN 1-4042-0756-2 (library binding)
1. Handicraft—Europe—History—To 1500—Juvenile literature. 2. Manors—Europe—History—Juvenile literature. 3. Middle Ages—-Europe—History—Juvenile literature. I. Netelkos, Jason. II. Title. III. Series: Jovinelly, Joann. Crafts of the Middle Ages. IV. Series.
TT55.J6727 2006
940.1—dc22

                                                                                    2006000401

47644 Apple 11/06

Manufactured in the United States of America

38179000669794

Note to parents
Some of these projects require tools or materials that can be dangerous if used improperly. Adult supervision will be necessary for projects that require the use of a craft knife, an oven, a stove top, or pins and needles. Before starting any of the projects in this book, you may want to cover your work area with newspaper or plastic. In addition, we recommend using a piece of thick cardboard to protect surfaces while cutting with craft or mat knives. We encourage you to discuss safety with your children and note in advance which projects may require your supervision.

CONTENTS

MEDIEVAL CULTURE

The Middle Ages spanned roughly from the fall of Rome in AD 476 to the beginning of the Renaissance after 1450. At the beginning of the Middle Ages, a distinctive social hierarchy known as feudalism emerged in western Europe. This social and economic system dominated the region that today encompasses the countries of England, France, Spain, and Germany.

The collapse of Roman leadership after centuries of successful domination marked a turning point in Europe. In fact, until recently, this decline of Roman scholarship and learning—the dawn of the Middle Ages—was considered a period of total isolation that discouraged learning. Historians once called this period the Dark Ages, but today's scholars instead consider this period a natural transition into the modern age.

The Roman Empire had been declining for hundreds of years before it fell. During this decline, the Romans had allowed various Germanic peoples into Roman territory, including Goths, Franks, and Lombards. The Romans accepted these outsiders largely to recruit them for their armies. They referred to them as "barbarians." Over time, more Germanic people invaded the empire from the north and east and adopted customs. Others rebelled, contributing to the empire's final collapse, and finally sacking the city of Rome at the beginning

A lord and noble watch while peasants plant vines and pick grapes in this fifteenth-century illumination from a manuscript about agricultural methods. Advancements in farming during the Middle Ages supported an increasing European population.

of the fifth century. Without any central governing system, new and competing political kingdoms emerged.

Among the only unifying factors that outlined the medieval lifestyle for all people was Christianity. Formally made the official religion of the Romans before the empire fell, Christianity dominated the subsequent medieval period. It influenced the way society was organized. Medieval rulers were considered divinely appointed. Kings and bishops owed their loyalty to the leader of the Roman Catholic Church, the pope. This system trickled down to the peasant farmer who owed his loyalty to a lord.

The feudal period peaked around 1100. Yet at its height, western Europe was made up of agricultural villages called manors. Their self-sufficient nature, organization of society by class, and ability to improve food production through agricultural innovations helped pave the way for Europe's first towns, the rebirth of trade and currency, and a new merchant middle class.

SEEKING PROTECTION

The social order of feudal society developed gradually and out of necessity, since the conditions in western Europe were chaotic and unstable. With their progress slowed by internal strife, political corruption, epidemics, and civil war, weakened Roman armies could no longer defend the empire's borders.

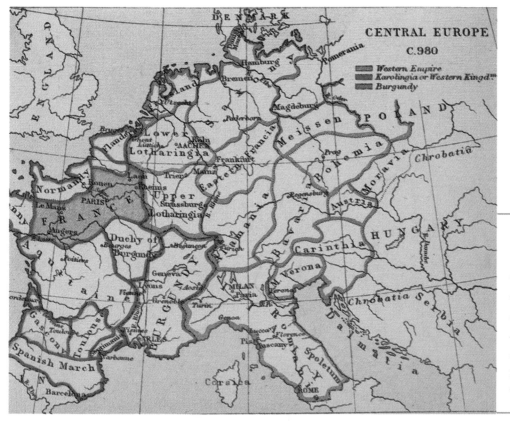

The kingdoms of central Europe are outlined in this map that indicates divisions of land around AD 980. After the decline of the Roman Empire, European kingdoms each competed for as much land and wealth as possible.

People wanted protection from Eastern invading groups, especially the Goths. Other invaders, such as the Vikings, came from the north. These seafaring people from Scandinavia posed a constant menace in communities along the coast. Muslim warriors invaded from points as far away as the Middle East and North Africa, spreading Islam. This continuous threat of invasion made people increasingly fearful. Small farmers began the custom of placing their lands and families under the protection of powerful landowners. Once the decision was made to request this defense, the title of ownership to the small farmer's land was transferred to the lord in exchange for his protection. The noble then granted back to the farmer temporary use of the land (until the farmer's death). This arrangement was an old Roman custom called precarium. Another Roman custom that would carry over was patronicium, where a noble gave land to a man in exchange for his military service.

Some landowners also gave up their use of excess lands to homeless or bankrupt farmers. In both instances, farmers were grateful for the security and looked to their landowners as lords. These arrangements continued as farmers could not rely upon Roman

armies, and, over time, land became more consolidated.

The formal ceremony in which feudal relationships were entered into was called commendation. The individuals commended themselves, or became vassals, to their lord.

FEUDALISM

As time passed, the Germanic groups eventually settled in different European regions. People cared less about protection than they did about farming the land and improving their livelihood. As the Middle Ages unfolded, feudal relationships were passed down. The basic hallmarks of feudalism were that lands were granted to barons, lords, knights, and vassals in exchange for their military service and loyalty.

In the feudal system, people were born into permanent positions in society. They were either a part of the noble class, such as the lords (or barons) who were given land grants by kings, or peasants and serfs who worked the land. The only exception to these divisions was a third branch of society, the people who were part of the church, such as monks, abbots, priests, and bishops. Nobles called barons wielded the most power, second only to bishops, religious leaders who ruled over regions called dioceses, usually situated around a cathedral within a city.

A lord or baron was a wealthy nobleman who received a land grant called a fief (or feudum) directly from a king. This fief was normally in the form of a manor, a large house or mansion with surrounding farmlands and pastures. Land on the manor was usually divided into sections, which the peasants cultivated under the lord's direction, and the demesne, a plot of land owned directly by the lord. The demesne was cared for by peasants.

Lords were well trained as knights and took special vows to protect the kings they served. For example, in 1066, when William of Normandy conquered England, he ordered a variety of castles built to protect and defend his armies from the Anglo-Saxons, which he had subdued. Within a few years, he gave about 180 honors (castles and land) to barons, who in turn gave part of their land to knights. He then had about 5,000 knights at his disposal for any military campaign. It is in this way that medieval armies were organized.

A vassal was any person who commended themselves to someone of a higher ranking and was given land or use of land in a feudal relationship. Peasants, vassals to the lords they served, were offered a plot of land to farm in exchange for their lord's protection. This agreement was sealed in a sworn ceremony called homage where the peasants placed their hands in the hands of their lords and took an oath of fealty, or loyalty. Once the agreement was made, it could not be broken.

Knights, who held a higher social status than peasants, owed military service to their lords. Usually, a vassal's military service was for a predetermined period, such as forty days per year. At the same time, lords owed fealty to ruling kings in exchange for gifts of land.

Although they were mostly in the rural countryside of Europe, lower peasants known as serfs also lived on the lord's manor. Serfs could not leave the land they lived on, nor could they leave their lord's service. In this class system, nobles never had to farm their own land. They only had to protect their workers and offer repayment in excess crops. This social structure was especially effective in France from about AD 800. In other parts of southern Europe, such as Italy, feudalism never fully took hold.

THE MANOR

The word "manor" comes from the French verb *maneir*, meaning "to

HIC·EST·VVAD ARD·   hIC·COQV TVR·CARO

This is a detail of the Bayeux Tapestry, *an eleventh-century embroidery that expressed visually the conquest of England by the Normans after* AD *1066. In this section, a lord on horseback instructs his subjects about farming methods.*

dwell." Usually, manors were large estates, roughly 900 to 2,000 acres (350 to 800 hectares), designed with various areas set aside for different purposes. In addition to the lord's mansion was his demesne. The manor also contained a parish church, small cruck houses or huts for the peasants, barns, a mill for grinding grain, orchards, woodlands, fishponds, an outdoor oven for baking, small herb and vegetable gardens, and a place for keeping bees.

The manor was divided into five basic parts: farmland, meadows, pastureland, woodlands, and the village. Beginning in AD 1000, farmland was organized in a three-field rotation system in order to keep the grounds fertile and avoid soil exhaustion. In the three-field system, one-third of the land set aside for farming was left fallow, or dormant, each season. This allowed

necessary nitrogen in the soil to be replaced. In this process of crop rotation, the fallow land changed each year, as did the other two crops. Although medieval farmers rotated crops, before the tenth century they were largely unaware of the farming technique of fertilization. For example, cattle manure was hauled away from the crops to a designated waste area.

Oxen were eventually replaced with horses, which were faster, and the heavy plow was developed. Before the invention of the heavy plow, most work had been done manually with rakes, spades, pitchforks, and scythes.

Meadows and pastureland were set aside to feed the lord's cattle and sheep, also cared for by peasants, and a defined woodland provided the manor with wood for building and fuel. Rabbits and deer were hunted for food.

Peasants ate little meat except for the occasional serving of chicken and pork (they were permitted to keep pigs, chickens, and sheep), as well as eggs and cheese. The staple of the peasant diet was grains and root vegetables. They also gathered a variety of nuts, berries, and other fruits. The sheep they kept were shorn to provide them with wool for clothing. In the center of the farmland was the village, located near a lake or stream. Firewood was gathered from a common pile, animals grazed on common meadows, and any surpluses of grain or wool were brought to town and sold.

Peasants fell into several distinctive groups in the feudal system. There were freemen, who owned their land outright and could leave the manor whenever they wanted. They could free their sons from the feudal system by sending them to a monastery, where they would have become monks. This was often a preferred lifestyle because it offered protection, education, and a steady diet.

Serfs, who were called villeins in England, were bound to the manor and could not leave their lord's service. A serf's parcel was normally about 30 acres (12 hectares). Serfs were never in fear of being unemployed, but they could also never improve their station

In this illumination, likely taken from a medieval Book of Hours, peasants are hard at work on a medieval manor. They are using oxen and a heavy plow (one of the most significant agricultural developments of the medieval period) to maintain the field.

in life. In theory, a lord was permitted to sell a serf's piece of land, along with the serf and his or her families, but this rarely occurred. A lord could also marry his serfs to whomever he chose and separate families. Most serfs accepted their lot in life, though a few sought their freedom. Those who did often fled to distant towns.

PEASANT LIFE

The life of a peasant was extremely difficult. Both men and women worked from sunrise to sunset. Men toiled in the fields, working their lord's demesne for three days a week before tending to their own land. They walked behind their oxen, cutting the land in a ridge-and-furrow pattern. They had to harvest all of the crop yields on a strict schedule that did not allow for sickness or leisure. In return for working the lord's demesne, serfs occasionally received a small portion of the crop yield. When cutting wood from trees, for example, a serf was often entitled to cut whatever branches he could reach by a hooked pole.

Women worked the fields and cared for the vegetable gardens near family cruck houses or huts. They also made clothing out of wool, which was cut from manor sheep, spun into yarn, and then woven into cloth. Women also sewed clothing from linen, which was produced from flax grown on manor land. They cared for the children and cooked meals. They also gathered fruit and nuts, brought grain to the lord's mill to be ground into flour, and dough to the lord's oven to be baked.

Peasants had few personal belongings, short of the clothing on their backs. Their diet was poor, lacking in iron, and could be made worse due to crop failure. And even if they were hungry, they were still forced to give away food to their lord as payment for his land.

Peasants, whether they were free or not, were required to report to the manor's manager, called the steward or seneschal. This gentleman reported back to the lord about the day-to-day progress on the manor and could inflict punishments on the peasants if they stopped working. These punishments might have included flogging, or beating with a whip. Any simple action might have cost the peasant a fee to his lord, such as being prohibited from grinding grain in the lord's mills or allowing cattle to graze on the lord's land. In addition, all peasants were required to pay 10 percent of their seasonal crops to the church, called tithe.

FEUDALISM IN DECLINE

As the agricultural revolution took hold, and fewer peasants were needed to work the land, more migrated to towns. Many fled the manors and became free. Some of these former farmers became merchants who traveled with their wares from town to town or to medieval fairs. Some of the fairs

This illumination is from Marco Polo's Book of Marvels, *in which the Venetian traveler and author describes a medieval town. Once inside the town walls, he describes a variety of laborers, including a carpenter, mason, and shopkeeper. Polo traveled extensively and wrote about his trips to Asia for medieval audiences.*

were famous throughout Europe. In times of good international relations, merchants from North Africa, Russia, Scandinavia, and the Middle East were all represented. Europeans began developing a desire for luxury goods. Before long, there was enough of a demand for some of these goods that artisans could establish businesses. More and more, feudal lifestyles faded. Villages on manors grew into towns.

With the rise of food production after the agricultural revolution, it became more profitable to transport surplus food from the manors to nearby towns. Traveling farmers and tradesmen were among the first medieval merchants. Soon, currencies were being minted and banks were formed. Nobles had an increased desire to acquire foreign goods, such as textiles and spices. Within a century, this desire for imported items helped support flourishing economies and overseas trade. As this changing world unfolded, a new group of people was introduced into society: the merchant middle class.

Life in a Medieval Manor

The general idea of a manor was that it remained completely self-sufficient without any outside interference. Its crops needed to adequately support a lord, his family, and the peasants who worked the land. Nearly everything was made from materials that were grown and harvested within the manor. Animals were kept and bred for eating and for providing wool, ponds provided fish, trees were cut for fuel and building, and grains such as oats, barley, and wheat were made into flour for baking. Honey was collected from beehives (sugar was not yet available). Some manors even had a wine or oil press. The only items that were brought into the manor were iron for forging tools and salt for preserving meat.

Manors were run according to the seasons, and the work was systematic. Peasants knew exactly what work had to be done from day to day and season

In this manuscript illumination, groups of peasants work the manorial land with scythes and rakes while the lord of the manor courts his lady. Although the lord had his own farmland on the manor, he was not required to do farm work.

to season. In the spring, the land was plowed and sowed for planting. The summer months were a time for tending crops and weeding, shearing the sheep, cutting and storing hay for the winter months, and preserving food. The annual harvest took place in the late summer and early fall. This was a time when grain was threshed and stored. Usually the winter was the best time for making tools and clothing, and doing repairs. If food was scarce that year, work was limited in order to conserve energy. During these times, peasants often slept more in order to forget their hunger.

Peasants had two types of land on a manor. Each had a plot, with a hut, garden, and space to keep animals. They also had a big field for growing crops such as grain. This land was farmed by all the peasants on the manor and was divided into strips. Each peasant also knew which areas on the manor were acceptable to gather wood or food, or on which to let their animals graze. To ignore these boundaries and encroach upon a lord's land was punishable by the lord according to his wishes.

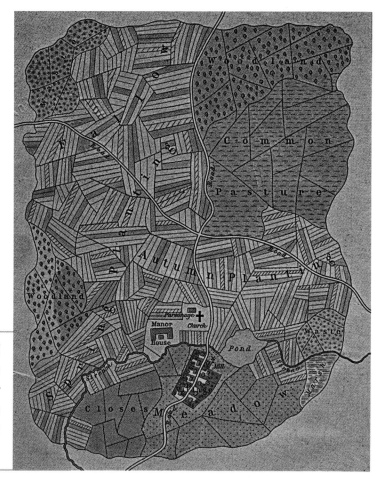

This map shows land divisions on a medieval manor between fertile and fallow plots as well as common lands and the demesne, or land owned only by the lord. Even though the demesne and its crops belonged to the lord, it was taken care of by peasants.

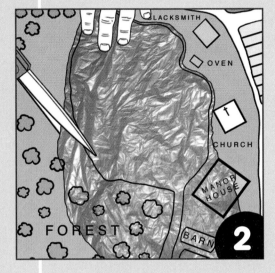

Miniature Manor

Imagine you are the lord of the manor and it's your job to divide the land. What percentage of it will be the lord's demesne and what percentage of it will be peasant farmland?

YOU WILL NEED

- Pizza box
- Masking tape
- Marker
- Glue
- Scissors
- Blue plastic bag
- Sand
- Soil
- Twigs
- Air-dry clay
- String
- Toothpicks
- Reindeer moss (lichen)
- Dried moss
- Pebbles
- Modeling clay
- Cardboard pieces
- Straw
- Paint

Step 1

Cut the lid off of the pizza box, but retain its sides. Close all four sides and reinforce them with masking tape. With a marker, draw a map of how you want your manor to be arranged. Include three fields (one of them is dormant), a common pasture, an orchard, a meadow, a forest, paths, a pond, and a stream. Mark areas where you will place the manor house, farmhouse, blacksmith, mill, church, and peasant houses.

Step 2

Spread glue inside your pond and stream areas and set a cut piece of a blue plastic bag into it. Press firmly and cut away the excess plastic. Don't worry if the plastic wrinkles.

Step 3

Cut pieces of dried moss to fit inside the areas that you've marked for your forest and meadow. Take small twigs and press them through the moss. Hold

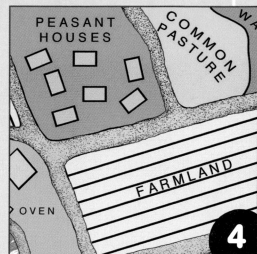

them in place with a ball of modeling clay, as shown. Attach the moss and the twigs to your box with the clay balls. To turn these twigs into trees, dab glue onto the tip of each twig and set a small piece of reindeer moss (lichen) onto it.

Step 4
Cover the entire area of your paths with glue. Sprinkle sand onto the glue and lightly press the sand with your fingers. Glue sand around your pond.

Step 5
Glue straw or soil to the box in the sections for your three fields. At least one-third of all the farmlands on a manor were a part of the lord's demesne.

Step 6
Use your imagination to add details that decorate your landscape. Make small buildings with clay using simple shapes. A wattle fence can be made by gluing cut toothpicks to make posts and weaving string to join them together. A small strip of cardboard covered with glued rocks can be a bridge. Add as much or as little detail as you'd like.

A Life of Toil

While the lord and his family lived inside a large house, mansion, or even a castle made of stone, his peasants lived in small, drafty, one- or two-room houses or huts on the manor. These structures were grouped together, though far enough apart to have a small plot of land to grow vegetable and herb gardens.

Since the roofs of these buildings were often high, small lofts for sleeping or storage were sometimes fashioned inside them. Most had a dirt floor and a pit in the center for a fire that provided heat and cooked meals. (Smoke from the fire was released through a hole in the roof.) During winter months, animals were sometimes penned inside the house in a corner.

To build these structures, peasants sunk posts in the ground and made walls by weaving flexible branches between them. This was called wattling, and it was also the process for making a type of fence that was used to cage animals like pigs and chickens. Stout stone walls

In this illumination from the late Middle Ages, French peasants try to warm themselves during winter. This period in history is sometimes referred to as the "Little Ice Age" because temperatures dropped significantly for several decades.

acted as a foundation to support woven branches that were covered with daub— a mixture of clay and chopped straw and cow hair. Adding the daub made the branches somewhat fireproof and helped seal drafts. In a few cases, peasants'

Medieval men, including a carpenter (left), physician with his patient (center), and blacksmith (right), are shown performing various job-related duties in this manuscript illumination from the fourteenth century. As the medieval period progressed, so did the specialization of many fields.

homes were made entirely with wood, but this was rare. Wooden timbers did, however, frame interior walls that were also partially made from wattle and daub. These buildings were usually finished in vertical wood siding. Windows were narrow, open slits in the walls, and roofs were thatched.

Peasants rarely left the manor where they were born. They spent the majority of their time working for their lords. Only about three days a week were spent farming their own land and small gardens. The demesne they farmed for their lord, as well as their individual parcels, were spread throughout the manor. All farmland was divided in long strips and then further divided into thirds so that the crops were rotated. It was in this way that everyone got an equal share of soil that was either fertile or fallow.

Some peasants were not farmers, however. Lords regularly employed peasants to

do a variety of other jobs around the manor, too. They worked as bakers, tanners, blacksmiths, potters, and so forth. Eventually, some of these peasants became merchants. A new middle class emerged when the feudal system waned in the twelfth century.

Peasants' homes tended to vary in design and materials depending on the region where they were built, but most looked like this basic one-room structure with a thatched roof. This is a reproduction of a peasant house that was built in Scotland.

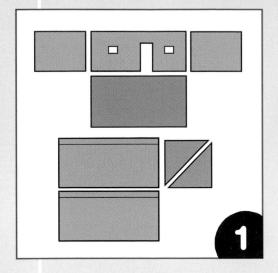

1

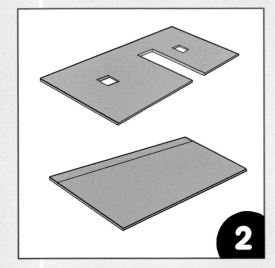

2

3

Peasant House

A peasant's house had few luxuries. Still, peasants were able to make good use of the raw materials they found on the manor.

YOU WILL NEED

- Cardboard
- Ruler and pencil
- Craft knife
- Masking tape
- Glue
- String
- Scissors
- White and brown paint
- Bowl, glue/water mixture, and newspaper strips (for papier-mâché)
- Paintbrushes

Step 1

For the front and floor of the house, cut two 9½ x 4-inch pieces of cardboard. Cut two 4 x 5-inch pieces for the sides. For the roof, cut two 9½ x 4½-inch pieces and one 4-inch square for the roof's sides. Cut the square in half to make two triangles, one for each side of the roof.

Step 2

With your ruler and craft knife, cut a doorway and windows in the front wall of the house. Score a ½-inch border along the top of the front and back roof pieces.

Step 3

With masking tape, attach the two roof pieces along the top of the scored edge and tape one triangle piece to each side. Tape the sides of the house to its front and floor. Tape the roof to the house.

Step 4

Dip paper strips into glue-and-water mixture, and cover the entire structure with a layer of papier-mâché. Smooth away excess water and bubbles with

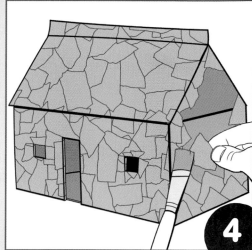

a paintbrush. This will reinforce the structure and give a nice texture to the walls. Allow to fully dry.

Step 5
To simulate a thatched roof, take bundles of string, about 2 inches in length, and tie them together in the middle. Fold the string at the knot and cover in watered-down brown paint. Make plenty of these painted bundles. The string should dry in the same direction.

Step 6
Paint the walls of your house with a thick layer of white paint. Starting at the bottom of the roof, glue the bundles of painted string in rows until the entire roof is covered. Decorate the inside of the house as you desire.

Working the Land

Peasants began to realize they needed to rotate their crops. They began growing summer crops in one section, fall crops in another, and leaving one fallow. This helped to avoid exhausting the soil, even if they were unaware of the need for nitrogen in the soil. (In some cases, the fallow field was the one where animals were allowed to graze and their manure was spread throughout the field the following season, though this was an irregular practice.) Near the coasts, farmers gathered seaweed and spread it on the fields. Peasants often spread bits of spoiled vegetables like lettuce and turnip pieces on the fields as a sort of composting. Growing a variety of crops and repositioning them regularly also helped control pests and disease.

Crops varied from year to year, though grains such as wheat and rye (to make flour for baking bread) and

Peasants are seen working in each square of this fifteenth-century calendar. Each month of the year was set aside for specific jobs and chores around the manor, with the coldest months used for indoor activities such as making repairs or mending clothing.

barley (to brew ale) were always planted. Oats were successful in colder climates, while warmer climates produced grapes for wine and olives for pressing olive oil. Most manors also contained fruit orchards where apples and pears were commonly grown. Lemons and oranges, which were introduced to Europeans by the Muslims during the religious wars known as the Crusades, were cultivated in warmer climates. Nearly every peasant grew his own onions, leeks, garlic, lettuce, peas, beans, beets, and pumpkins.

Throughout the year, peasants and their children combed the forest for supplies. Twigs, branches, pine needles and cones, acorns, moss, and dried leaves were all useful for weaving, for building, or as fire starters. Acorns were fed to pigs to help fatten them. Wild honey was taken to sweeten pottage and pies. At various times, peasants carried bags to gather all of these items as well as wild mushrooms, berries and other fruits, and chestnuts and walnuts, all food that was found in the forest. Foraging for food, especially if crops had been ruined or the return was too low, was a must during medieval times. Chestnuts were a mainstay of the French diet during this period.

This fourteenth-century fresco depicts an Italian manorial estate flanked by a vineyard and olive groves. Unlike in France and England, kingdoms in Italy were less drawn into the feudal system.

Besides planting, peasants spent much of their time harvesting crops. Peasants also made use of common areas on the manor where they forged for nuts, berries, and fruit. It is for this reason that many of them carried bags as part of their daily attire.

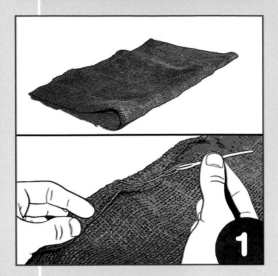

Peasant Sack

Peasants often used plain sacks to gather fruit, vegetables, mushrooms, and chestnuts, and to carry tools with them into the field.

YOU WILL NEED
- **Burlap**
- **String**
- **Heavy twine**
- **Plastic yarn needle**
- **Scissors**

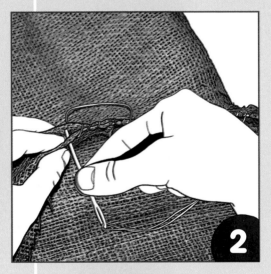

Step 1
Take a large square of burlap and fold it in half vertically. Sew the edges together with string. For best results, fold both edges back before sewing.

Step 2
Turn the burlap inside out and cut a round piece of burlap to fit on the bottom of your sack. Make the round piece slightly larger than you think you would need.

Step 3
Cut any excess burlap from the bottom.

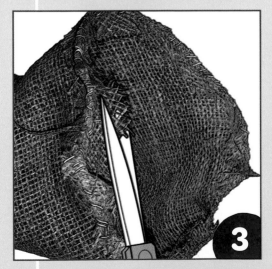

Step 4
Fold the opening of your sack about 1½ inches along the top edge to make a flap that goes around the entire sack. Make a large hole in this flap and thread a long piece of twine through the hole and around the bag so that the end of the twine comes out the same hole. Tie the ends into a knot to make a loop.

Step 5
Sew the flap to the sides of the sack, trapping the twine in between.

Step 6
Now your sack has a working pull-string and it's ready for you to use to gather fruits and vegetables.

Working in the Mill

Windmills have been in use since ancient times, as has the technology of grinding grain into flour with large millstones. However, windmills were first used in Europe during the Middle Ages. When windmills were referenced in medieval records and documents, they were often just called mills. They were powered naturally by wind and water or manually by human or animal labor. Mills were constructed and maintained by millwrights and were continually improved upon during the medieval period, especially by the Dutch.

Watermills were as popular as windmills at the same time, if not more so. Both were used to power gears that helped turn large, heavy millstones to create flour from grain and to power triphammers, the massive hammers that were used in the iron forges for beating hot metal into thin sheets.

Most every manor had a system of fresh water that was used for drinking, washing, fishing, and to power mills like those seen in this thirteenth-century French manuscript illumination. Pictured here is a medieval water-powered grain mill.

Mills were also used to pound and soften fabrics, provide power for saws, make paper, and press olives.

In most cases, the local lord owned the mill and charged a fee for its use. Because everyone needed flour for baking, owning any type of mill was lucrative. Village peasants carried their grain to the mill and paid a fee in the form of eggs or other crops to grind their

finus & afellus afedendo dictuf. qi afe
duf. fed hoc nomen ad magif ecuuifco

grain. Eventually, commoners got together and invested in commercial mills. Buying and selling shares of these structures was an early form of investing. Shares in the mills were often inherited, and their value went up and down over time depending on the mills' condition, the overall demand for their service, and their ability to run properly.

Medieval windmills were constructed on top of a structure that could be moved manually around a massive pivot, or post, toward the wind as it changed direction. Post mills like this appeared in the twelfth century and were manually turned with a tail pole or tiller beam to face whichever direction the wind was blowing. This was done either by a group of men or oxen. Once the mill was positioned toward the wind, its gears were set in motion and the millstones ground grain into flour. The only control to this device was a manual brake. Other period mills were known as smock mills, similar to post mills but with a fixed wooden body, or tower mills, similar to smock mills but with a body made from brick or stone.

Windmills like this one were developed in twelfth-century Europe and were improved over subsequent decades, especially by the Dutch. Although they were not terribly efficient, they did help replace animal power in regular grain production.

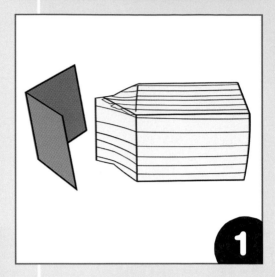

1

2

3

Windmill

Windmills such as this post mill were common throughout Europe during the Middle Ages, especially in the north.

YOU WILL NEED
- Pint-size milk carton
- Scrap cardboard
- Masking tape
- Chopsticks
- Bamboo skewers
- Matchsticks
- Oven-bake clay
- 4 recycled teabags
- Large thread spool
- Glue
- Awl
- Scissors
- Paint/painbrush

Step 1
Cover the surface of your milk carton with overlapping strips of masking tape. Cut and fold a piece of cardboard to fit snugly on top of the carton with sides that hang over like a roof. Glue this piece to the top of the carton, as shown.

Step 2
Glue your thread spool to the bottom center of the carton, as shown. Hold the spool in place with masking tape until the glue sets. To make the base, cut a 5-inch square of cardboard. With your awl, make a hole in the center of the square. Cut 1½ inches off the pointed tip of a chopstick and glue the piece you cut off into the hole. The thread spool will rest on this stick.

Step 3
Next, take your awl and make a large hole in the center of the front of your mill, about 2½ inches from the top. Make another hole in the back of the carton that is aligned with the front hole. Insert the rest of your chopstick through both of these holes. Take a small ball of clay and flatten it into a disc. Press the clay into the end of the chopstick to make an imprint in the clay.

Step 4

Cut four bamboo skewers
into 6-inch pieces
with scissors.
Gently press
the skewers into the
clay, as shown. These skewers will later be made into sails.
Remove the skewers and the chopstick from the clay,
and bake the clay according to package directions.
When baking is complete, set aside to cool.

Step 5

To make the sails, glue two vertical matchsticks 1 inch
apart, onto the edge of your teabag paper, as shown.
Glue the bamboo skewer in the center of the matchsticks so that the tops of all three sticks are aligned.
Cut and glue smaller matchstick pieces to your sails
as support bars. After all four sails are complete, set
them aside to dry. Once dry, cut the excess paper
away from the sails with scissors.

Step 6

Glue the clay piece onto the chopstick and glue the
sails into the holes of the clay, as shown. You can add
detail to your windmill by cutting and gluing more
matchsticks to make windows. Paint as you desire.

Medieval Diet

Despite periods of famine, medieval diets had a great deal of variety and were not filled with spoiled food as is sometimes believed. When food was abundant, any excess was stored for use during the winter months when fresh food was no longer available. People of nobility obviously had a more lavish diet than did the peasants. Lords and their families enjoyed meat and fish regularly and kept a variety of animals on the manor for just that purpose. Many people of noble backgrounds enjoyed pheasant, pigeon, peacock, rabbit, deer, and a variety of fish. Nobles were also known to have feasts of many courses and commonly had a glass of wine with their large midday meal. They also tasted imported delicacies that would have been unheard of to peasants, such as rice, dried dates and apricots, and pistachios.

A group of peasants takes a break from farming in this painting by Pieter Brueghel the Younger. Many times were lean during the medieval period, so peasants commonly gained protein by eating nuts and grain-based porridges instead of meat and fish.

The peasant diet was far less exciting, though both classes were limited to what was available during various times throughout the year. Peasants rarely ate meat and fish, though these were enjoyed during special occasions and feast days. They instead gained protein from beans, eggs, cheese, and nuts. Bread, especially

dark, course loaves, was also a staple food. When flour was unavailable, bread was made with beans. Pork in the form of bacon was sometimes eaten, as were fruits and vegetables during the summer and fall. Cakes and puddings were sometimes enjoyed as well.

Many peasants would have regularly eaten pottage, a form of thick porridge often made with boiled grain. Barley, oats, and wheat were all used to make pottage, as were chestnuts, which were sometimes mixed with warm milk and honey for a sweet treat. Sometimes pottage was made with vegetables or with meat or fish scraps, and it was common to toss herbs in the pot for added flavor. In some cases, a kettle of pottage remained on the fire for several days. Ingredients were added as they became available and the thick, soupy meal was in steady supply to feed growing families and guests. Most peasants drank ale with their meals since their limited water supply was often contaminated. Ale also provided much-needed carbohydrates for the peasants who labored in the fields all day.

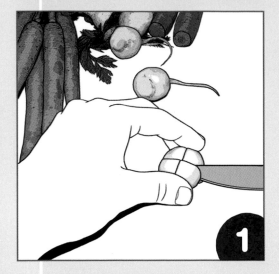

Vegetable Pottage*

Pottage was a meal enjoyed by most peasants during the Middle Ages, especially since they maintained small vegetable gardens. Pottage was sometimes made richer with ground grains, beans, or nuts. This vegetable pottage is based on an actual medieval recipe.

"Take turnips and wash them clean, quarter them, boil them, take them up. Cast them in a good broth and see them; mince onions and cast them with saffron and salt, and mess it forth with powder douce."

—from Curye on Inglysch: English Culinary Manuscripts of the Fourteenth Century

* ADULT SUPERVISION IS ADVISED FOR THIS RECIPE

YOU WILL NEED
- 2-quart saucepan
- Mixing bowls, spoon, cutting board, knife
- Potato masher
- 2 cups of mixed turnips and carrots, cleaned and quartered
- 1 cup of minced onions (one large onion)
- 1½ cup of chicken broth
- Pinch of saffron
- Pinch of salt
- Powder douce (2 teaspoons honey [white or brown sugar can be substituted], ⅜ teaspoon cinnamon, ⅜ teaspoon ginger)

Step 1
Wash and quarter carrots and turnips. Boil them over medium heat for 5 to 8 minutes.

Step 2
When the vegetables are cooked through (insert a fork to see if they are soft), drain the water and return them to the saucepan. Return the saucepan to the stove, but don't turn it on.

Step 3
Mince one large onion into tiny pieces. Put the pieces in a small bowl and set aside. Add the minced onion and

chicken broth to the vegetables. Mix. Add a pinch of salt and a pinch of saffron. Cover and allow vegetables to simmer on a low setting for 15 to 20 minutes, or until broth has slightly evaporated.

Step 4
In a small bowl, mix your powder douce: cinnamon, ginger, and honey or sugar. Add this mixture to the vegetables as they simmer, stirring occasionally.

Step 5
Remove from heat. With a potato masher, gently mash any large vegetable pieces.

Step 6
Serve hot with bread. This recipe yields enough for four small servings.

Safekeeping

This is the main room of a fourteenth-century manor house, the equivalent of a castle's great hall. Some manor homes were simple and plain, though others took the size and appearance of mansions or castles.

Both peasants and nobles had few personal belongings. It wasn't until around the thirteenth century that people desired luxury items on a larger scale. These things included items such as carpets from the Middle East (which were hung on the wall or draped across tables since they were considered too fine to keep on the floor), silk fabrics, jewelry, and ceramics. Any such items for a lord and his family had to be imported into the manor. Nobles had some furniture, slept in beds with mattresses, and had changes of clothing. Most had jewelry, belts, gloves, a variety of hats, shoes, and utensils and other tableware. Some even owned items made of glass, which were quite rare. By comparison, they owned far more than an average peasant.

Peasants owned very few items. They might have had a second set of clothing, but they wore the mud-caked garments on their backs until they were all but threadbare. Most walked around barefoot in the spring and summer months, especially in the fields while they worked. Some had cloth shoes or clogs that they certainly wore in the winter to protect their feet from the cold. Most usually had a hat. Most also had a cup and perhaps a bowl that they would take to the manor house on feast days.

Some peasants had a child's cradle (made of birch wood for good luck, since a third of the children died before their first birthday), perhaps crudely made beds for themselves, and small stools for seating. Benches were also commonly used with a small table. Another kind

of bench was called a settle. A settle had a back and sides and looked somewhat like a church pew does today. Any small items were kept in chests for safekeeping and could be grabbed quickly during times of trouble, such as during a raid or fire. Chests were also used as luggage when a person traveled or went on a pilgrimage.

Chests were common in the Middle Ages, and they served duel purposes. Not only were they used for storage by all classes, but they also made good seating. They came in all shapes and sizes. Some were very plain, while others were decorated ornately. Some chests were made from boards that were up to nine feet (about three meters) in length, while others could be very small, like modern jewelry boxes. Most were carved wood with leather or iron straps to keep them closed. Some even had locks. A few that were made for nobility to store royal treasure were completely made of iron. Priests also used chests inside the church for storing vestments. Anything of value was kept sealed away in a chest until it was needed.

This is a wooden chest from England that dates from the thirteenth century. Nearly every family owned at least one wooden chest, which was used for storage and seating.

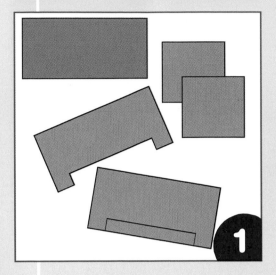

Storage Chest

Both lords and peasants commonly stored valuables in small chests that could be grabbed quickly during a raid or battle.

YOU WILL NEED

- Cardboard
- Ruler
- Pen
- Craft knife
- Masking tape
- Two 12" x 12" cork sheets
- Paper fastening brads
- Glue
- Straight pins
- Brown craft paint
- Paintbrush

Step 1

Cut three 10 x 5-inch rectangles from cardboard to make the front, back, and bottom of your storage chest. Cut two 4½ x 5-inch pieces for the sides. With your ruler and pen, draw a line along the bottom of both the front and back pieces, about 1 inch from the edge. Cut out this 7 inch space, about 1½ inch from each corner, to make "legs" for your chest, as shown.

Step 2

Next, take the cardboard front and back pieces and trace them onto sheets of cork. Cut them out using your ruler and craft knife. Cut 5 x 6-inch pieces of cork for the sides of the chest and a 10½ x 6-inch piece for its lid.

Step 3

Tape the sides of your cardboard chest to the bottom cardboard piece, making an open box.

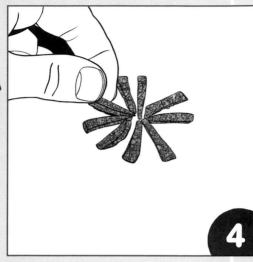

Step 4
Using scrap pieces of cork, you can cut and glue designs for the front of your storage chest, as shown.

Step 5
Glue the cork sides to the sides of the cardboard construction. Hold the edges together with straight pins until the glue sets.

Step 6
To attach the lid to your chest, cut two 1 x 2½-inch pieces of cardboard and make matching holes through the cardboard and the edge of the lid and the cardboard and the back of the chest. Attach the cardboard hinge with paper fasteners. When finished, remove the straight pins and paint your chest with brown craft paint.

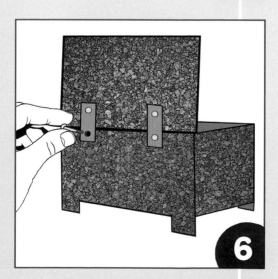

Recreation

Nobles are pictured on a dais (right) *while peasants gather in the manor house for festivities and dancing. Musicians play their instruments from a balcony perched high above the scene.*

Peasants had little time for leisure, but they did enjoy time away from the fields. Their work was strenuous, but they were fortunate enough to enjoy a variety of holidays, most of them religious. Each season of the year offered various religious holidays when work completely ceased. During these lively times, peasants enjoyed lavish feasts at the manor hosted by their lord. Meat, fish, cakes, and other sweets were served. They also played a variety of games, and drinking ale was common.

Celebrations and feasts at the manor were most common during the Christmas holidays. They took place over a fortnight, a period of two weeks between Christmas Eve, December 24, to Epiphany, January 6. The first Monday after Epiphany was known as Plow Day, and peasants played games in the field such as racing each other with their plows. Other holidays were Candlemas (February 2), Shrove Tuesday (the last day before Lent, the forty days preceding Easter), May Day (May 1), and Whitsunday (the Christian Pentecost, or fifty days after the resurrection of Jesus Christ). Saint John's Day was celebrated on June 24, and Lammas (August 1) marked the end of the hay harvest. Other holidays were Christian feast days, holy days, or days set aside to celebrate various saints.

A variety of games and other pastimes helped relieve peasants of the monotony of their backbreaking work. Most sang in the fields while they farmed. Children and adults enjoyed

games like blind man's bluff and tag, and sports such as wrestling, swimming, and football. Betting on cockfights was also common. Games involving dice were extremely popular. Although gambling was a vice that was frowned upon by the church, it was widespread nonetheless. People of all ages and classes played early board games such as backgammon, checkers, Fox and Geese, and Nine Man Morris, but chess was usually played only by nobility. Cards were introduced during the fourteenth century and quickly became wildly popular. Unfortunately, like dice, playing cards encouraged the act of gambling, so they were considered sinful.

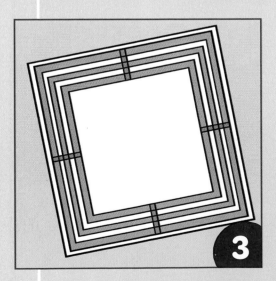

Nine Man Morris

Nine Man Morris, a popular medieval game of strategy for two players, was enjoyed by all classes of society, especially nobility. Although it is slightly similar to tic-tac-toe, it is far more challenging.

YOU WILL NEED

- **Cardboard**
- **2 different colors of oven-bake clay**
- **Ruler and pencil**
- **Craft knife**
- **Craft paint**

Step 1

Cut an 8-inch square piece of cardboard. Draw a ½-inch border around the square with a ruler and pencil.

Step 2

Draw three concentric squares, about a ½ inch apart.

Step 3

Draw four lines, one from the interior center of each square, that radiate outward to the third square.

Step 4

Next draw circles along each of your four extensions at points where they cross other lines, as shown. In the central square you can draw a medieval design of your choice, or you can paint it a solid color.

Step 5

Paint your concentric squares one color and the lines between them another color. Paint the circles in a third color. Roll small pieces of clay into balls and flatten them to make eighteen barrel-like game pieces. Make nine in one color, and nine in another. Bake the clay when finished.

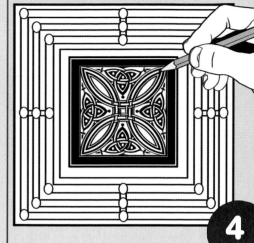

Step 6

To play, each player takes turns placing his or her nine game pieces on the board. If a player places three pieces in a straight row it's called forming a mill. Whenever a mill is formed, the player who succeeded in forming it gets to remove one of his opponent's game pieces. Once all the pieces have been placed, players take turns moving any one peg to a vacant, adjacent hole. If a player gets three pieces in a row, again, one of the opponent's pieces is removed.

Town Life

By the end of the fourteenth century, feudalism in French kingdoms was declining. Many peasants revolted against the system, as illustrated by this illumination that shows the killing of a French peasant. Other peasants fled the manors to growing towns and cities.

By the twelfth century, feudal systems and relationships in western Europe were widespread, but there was no longer enough arable land that could be cultivated. Feudalism had reached its peak. Feudal relationships started to break down as peasants moved away from manors and into towns. At the same time, the local lords' power began to decrease as kings centralized their administrations and control over their kingdoms. Members of the towns that had come into existence on the local lord's land began to petition the lords for a charter in order to create an autonomous government, in return for paying certain taxes and fees.

In 1215, English barons formed an alliance and wrote the Magna Carta (Great Charter). This document was an assertion of their rights, including their right to the land. The Magna Carta put limits on absolute royal law. It stated that the church was free to run itself. In this way, it acted to separate the church from the state. The Magna Carta laid down rules about limiting taxes paid to the king. It helped protect people from being taken advantage of for small offenses. It protected people's property from being taken, especially if they had debts. The charter eliminated "witnesses" of crimes that were paid by the government. It also created a civil grand jury so that a person had a right to a fair trial. The Magna Carta also created the idea of electing leaders to represent the people's needs and wishes.

The Magna Carta was an effort to create a reform movement in England that gave more power to the people and less to the royal king. In this case, it was King John (1166–1216). Today, the Magna Carta is seen as the first attempt to create a government of the people and the earliest parliamentary government in England. The Magna Carta is the first document concerning democratic principles that was ever created.

This image shows an early medieval English court in Westminster Hall in London. Chained prisoners are featured in the foreground.

This is a copy of the Magna Carta signed by King John of England. The Magna Carta helped lay the foundation for the future political and personal liberties of medieval towns as they developed.

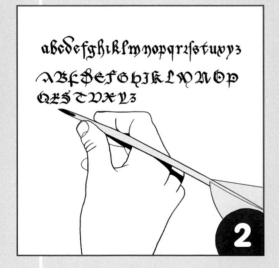

Magna Carta

Many manors were transformed into towns after the twelfth century. In order to become a town, lords needed permission from the king, who usually signed a charter. The basis for individual charters was the Magna Carta, or the Great Charter.

YOU WILL NEED

- Several goose quills (available at craft/art supply stores)
- Craft knife
- Bottled india ink
- Heavyweight paper
- Ruler and pencil
- Paints or markers
- Oven-bake clay
- Plastic bottle with cap
- Toothpick
- Small plastic figurine
- Ribbon
- Glue

Step 1

Carefully strip the feathers from your goose quills. Cut the tip of the rooted end in a diagonal with your craft knife. Notice the clear part of the center. This is where the ink will deposit when the quill is dipped in ink.

Step 2

Dip your quill in the bottle of ink and blot the excess ink on a paper towel. Practice writing on scrap paper before you begin your project. Familiarize yourself with the variety of designs that can be achieved with a quill pen. These vary from fine to thick lines.

Step 3

Decide what you want to write on your document. You can make your own version of the Magna Carta, like the one shown on the opposite page. Lightly draw a 2-inch border around your page with a ruler and pencil. Draw horizontal lines for text, as well as coats of arms. If this is a classroom project, you can make the coats of arms to represent individual classmates. Color the shields with paint or markers.

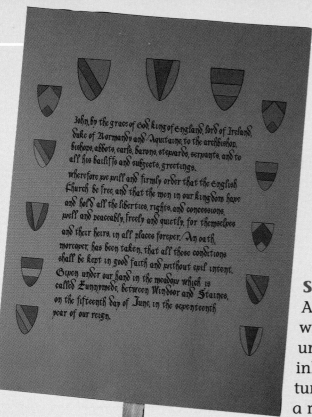

Step 4

After you have written your document and the ink has dried, turn it over. Glue a ribbon, approximately 10 inches long, to the center of the back of the page so that about 5 inches of it hangs over the bottom edge, as shown. To make a stamp for your seal, take a handful of oven-bake clay and form it into a ball.

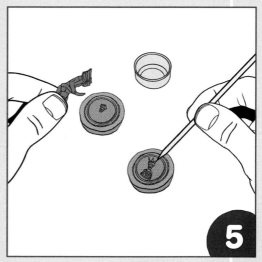

Step 5

Press a plastic bottle cap into the center of the clay ball to flatten it and make an impression. Next, make a smaller circle impression within a circle with the opening of the bottle itself. Draw a design within the smaller circle. You can use a small plastic figurine to make an impression of a face. If you want letters on your seal, be sure to write them backwards. When finished, bake the clay stamp according to package directions.

Step 6

After your "wax" seal stamp has cooled, take a small ball of clay and press it into the stamp. Remove the clay disc and bake it. When cool, glue it to the ribbon as shown.

TIMELINE

AD 313 Constantine imposes the Edict of Milan, preaching tolerance for Christianity.

410 Visigoths sack Rome.

circa 476 The Roman Empire falls.

476–1000 The period historians sometimes refer to as Europe's Dark Ages.

circa 700 Feudal system is established in France.

711 Muslims invade Spain.

768 Charlemagne becomes king of the Franks.

793 Beginning of Viking raids in England.

1066 William the Conqueror conquers England.

1095 Pope Urban II urges Christian knights to defend Christianity.

1096–1291 The Christian Crusades are launched to recapture the Holy Land from Muslims.

1161 First guilds are established; the era of cathedral-building begins.

1171 The Bank of Venice opens.

1179 The third Lateran Council decrees all cathedrals must have schools.

1180 Windmills first appear in Europe.

1215 The fourth Lateran Council requires Jews to wear identifying badges; signing of the Magna Carta.

1241 Mongols invade Europe.

1271 Marco Polo travels to Asia.

1300 Feudalism ends.

1314–1322 The great famine (alternate droughts and heavy rains in northern Europe).

1337–1453 Hundred Years' War between England and France.

1347–1530 The plague kills about 25 million people throughout Europe.

1381 Peasants' Revolt.

1453 The fall of Constantinople to Ottoman Turks (often taken as the end of the Middle Ages).

GLOSSARY

abbot The male leader of a monastery or abbey.

bailiff A powerful manor manager who answered directly to the lord.

bishop A high-ranking, powerful church official whose job was to oversee a diocese.

charter A written agreement or contract that outlined a town's area, its privileges, its authority to collect tolls and taxes, and its right to begin an independent government.

Crusades A series of religious wars fought between Christians and Muslims that occurred between 1096 and 1270.

Dark Ages An outdated term that is often used to describe the period of the Middle Ages because of its isolationism and illiteracy.

demesne A plot of farmland that belonged directly to a lord.

diocese A region controlled by a bishop that usually includes a city where a cathedral was located.

fallow Describes land that is uncultivated.

fealty Loyalty by a peasant to his or her lord.

feudalism A social and economic system that was based on land and power distribution where peasants and serfs worked for nobles in return for food and housing.

fief A plot of land given to a lord or peasant in exchange for service and loyalty.

hierarchy An arrangement of persons organized according to rank or authority.

homage A special ceremony where a young man becomes a knight.

knight A man-at-arms who served a lord.

lord A male knight and/or noble who was given a fief (plot of land) by a noble more powerful than himself.

reeve A peasant and farmer who helped manage the other peasants who worked on the lord's demense.

serf The lowest class of peasant laborer in the feudal system.

FOR MORE INFORMATION

The Metropolitan Museum of Art
1000 Fifth Avenue
New York, NY 10028-0198
(212) 535-7710
Web site: http://www.metmuseum.org

The Pierpont Morgan Library
29 East 36th Street
New York, NY 10016
(212) 685-0610
Web site: http://www.morganlibrary.org

WEB SITES

Due to the changing nature of Internet links, the Rosen Publishing Group, Inc., has developed an online list of Web sites related to the subject of this book. This site is updated regularly. Please use the link below to access the list:

http://www.rosenlinks.com/ccma/mema

FOR FURTHER READING

Bishop, Morris. *The Middle Ages.* Boston, MA: Houghton Mifflin Company, 1987.

Chrisp, Peter. *Town and Country Life* (Medieval Realms). San Diego, CA: Lucent Publishers, 2004.

Corbishley, Mike. *The Middle Ages* (Cultural Atlas for Young People). New York, NY: Facts on File, 2003.

Gies, Frances, and Joseph Gies. *Life in a Medival Village.* New York, NY: Harper and Row, 1991.

Gies, Joseph, and Frances Gies. *Life in a Medieval City.* New York, NY: Harper & Row, 1981.

Rowling, Marjorie. *Life in Medieval Times.* New York, NY: Penguin Putnam, 1973.

INDEX

ABOUT THE AUTHOR AND ILLUSTRATOR

Joann Jovinelly and Jason Netelkos have collaborated on many educational projects for young people. This is their second crafts series encouraging youngsters to learn history through hands-on projects. Their first series, Crafts of the Ancient World, was published by the Rosen Publishing Group in 2001. They live in New York City.

PHOTO CREDITS

Cover (center), p. 33 (bottom) Victoria & Albert Museum, London/Art Resource, NY; p. 4 HIP/Art Resource, NY; pp. 5, 13 (bottom) Courtesy of the University of Texas Libraries, The University of Texas at Austin; p. 8 Musee de la Tapisserie, Bayeux, France, with special authorization of the city of Bayeux/Bridgeman Art Library; p. 9 Victoria & Albert Museum, London, UK/Bridgeman Art Library; p. 11 © Oxford Science Archive/Heritage-Images/The Image Works; p. 12 The Art Archive/Torre Aquila Trento/Dagli Orti (A); pp. 13 (top), 40, 21 (bottom) British Library, London, UK/Bridgeman Art Library; p. 16 Musee Conde, Chantilly, France/UK/Bridgeman Art Library; p. 17 (top) © The British Library/HIP/ The Image Works; p. 17 (bottom) Graeme Cornwallis/Lonely Planet Images; p. 20 Reunion des Musees Nationaux/Art Resource, NY; p. 21 (top) akg-images/ Electa; pp. 24, 25 (top) The Granger Collection, New York; pp. 25 (bottom), 37 (bottom) © Gianni Dagli Orti/Corbis; p. 28 Giraudon/Art Resource, NY; p. 29 (top) Bildarchiv Preussischer Kulturbesitz/Art Resource, NY; p. 29 (bottom) Bibliotheque Nationale, Paris, France/Bridgeman Art Library; p. 32 akg-images/ A.F. Kersting; p. 33 (top) Erich Lessing/Art Resource, NY; p. 36 © Lebrecht Music & Arts/The Image Works; p. 37 (top) Art Resource, NY; p. 41 (top) Inner Temple, London, UK/Bridgeman Art Library; p. 41 (bottom) © Bettmann/Corbis. All crafts designed by Jason Netelkos and Joann Jovinelly. All craft illustrations by Jason Netelkos. All craft photography by Joann Jovinelly.

Special thanks to Christina Burfield for her continued support and encouragement.

Designer: Evelyn Horovicz; Editor: Leigh Ann Cobb
Photo Researcher: Gabriel Caplan/Nicole DiMella